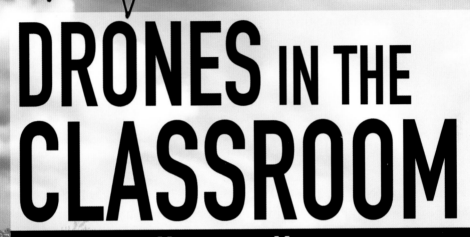

DRONES IN THE CLASSROOM

KATHERINE YAUN

ROSEN
PUBLISHING

New York

Published in 2017 by The Rosen Publishing Group
29 East 21st Street, New York, NY 10010

Copyright 2017 by The Rosen Publishing Group, Inc.

First Edition

Library of Congress Cataloging-in-Publication Data

Names: Yaun, Katherine, author.
Title: Drones in the classroom / Katherine Yaun.
Description: First edition. | New York, NY : Rosen Publishing, 2017. |
  Series: Inside the world of drones | Includes bibliographical references
  and index.
Identifiers: LCCN 2016029589 | ISBN 9781508173458 (library bound)
Subjects: LCSH: Drone aircraft in education—Juvenile literature. | Drone
  aircraft—Juvenile literature.
Classification: LCC LB1044.85 .Y38 2017 | DDC 371.33—dc23
LC record available at https://lccn.loc.gov/2016029589

Manufactured in China

CONTENTS

INTRODUCTION _____ 4

CHAPTER 1
UP IN THE AIR _____ 7

CHAPTER 2
SCIENCE, TECHNOLOGY, MATH,
AND ENGINEERING (STEM)_____ 17

CHAPTER 3
DRONES IN MEDIA AND THE HUMANITIES ___ 28

CHAPTER 4
OUTSIDE OF THE CLASSROOM_____ 38

CHAPTER 5
THE FUTURE OF DRONES IN EDUCATION ____ 49

GLOSSARY _____ 57
FOR MORE INFORMATION _____ 58
FOR FURTHER READING _____ 59
BIBLIOGRAPHY _____ 60
INDEX_____ 62

INTRODUCTION

A high school cross-country team is competing in a large cross-country tournament. Family members, friends, and classmates stand in the bleachers on either side of the finish line straining to see the school team members amid dozens of runners. A drone buzzes by. But it is not a police or military drone. This one is taking aerial photographs and video. The coach has arranged to get the drone-captured footage to present to her team Monday morning in order to review their race performance.

Later that week, over on the same high school's football field, a physics class is combining lessons in mathematics, engineering, physics, and design to test out the lightweight drones equipped with cameras that they have been working on all semester. They are eager to perfect the drones to win a school contest: the team that creates the lightest functioning model that can hover the longest and take the best photographs will win. In addition to a cash prize, the group's drone will be used that very night to help create a promotional film for the school's football team.

Drones have exploded onto the scene in recent years, finding their way into school-related activities and lessons. Today, drone technologies have the potential to revolutionize and improve multiple sectors including warfare, commerce, government, media production, and entertainment.

Given this variety, it is easy to see how drones can be useful in the classroom, too. Using or building a drone not

STUDENTS WHO BUILD OR OPERATE DRONES CAN LEARN HANDS-ON IN MANY SUBJECTS. HERE, STUDENTS USE A SMARTPHONE TO CONTROL THE DRONE THEY MADE.

only teaches lessons in subject areas like STEM (science, technology, engineering, and mathematics), but they are also useful aids for learning subjects as diverse as journalism, art, history, and photography.

In December 2015, nearly one million drones were purchased as gifts during the holiday shopping season in the United States. Even as drones' popularity is skyrocketing, concerns about their potential hazards are on the rise, too. In this book, we will learn what drones are, their benefits and potential dangers (to both individuals and to society), and how they can nonetheless support a range of educational lessons and school-related aims, from science education to securing your school building. We will also examine how the future of drones and your own future professional life will intersect in some expected and unexpected ways.

Students considering future careers in the military, law enforcement, arts and entertainment, commerce, or government are guaranteed to encounter drones in their work. They will need to understand the technical, ethical, and entrepreneurial issues surrounding them in order to make sound decisions. Ultimately, the more you learn about drones now, the more prepared you will be as a student and as a future professional. Drones have buzzed onto the scene and it is inevitable that you will come across this technology sooner or later. There are many reasons to be excited about the current and future use of drones in and outside the classroom.

CHAPTER 1

Up in the Air

People have been fascinated with flying vehicles for centuries. There is even evidence that ancient Egyptians created a very basic, rudimentary aircraft. In the late fifteenth century, famed artist Leonardo da Vinci is credited with designing the first helicopter, which he called the "aerial screw." Hot-air balloons were among the first manned and unmanned aerial vehicles. However, it wasn't until the Wright brothers' 1903 development and successful flight of an airplane that this dream of flight became a reality.

Regardless of whether the vehicle was an airplane, helicopter, manual glider, or balloon, for many years a pilot was required to accompany the aircraft during its flight in order to maneuver it safely and effectively. As early as 1917, however, engineers had discovered remote control technol-

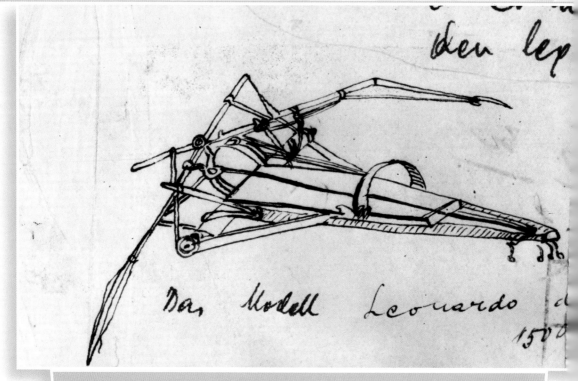

THIS ANCIENT SKETCH OF A FLYING MACHINE BY LEONARDO DA VINCI—DRAWN IN THE FIFTEENTH CENTURY—SHOWS THAT HUMANS HAVE BEEN FASCINATED WITH THE CONCEPT OF FLIGHT FOR A VERY LONG TIME.

ogy that allowed a person on the ground to maneuver an aircraft in the sky. This technology was quickly adopted by the world's militaries to carry out strikes during World War I. Ever since, it has been employed in other conflicts, and has been modified for use in commerce, agriculture, visual media, and more.

In the last 50 years, toy manufacturers have developed remote-controlled airplanes and helicopters. Meanwhile, scientists and engineers have developed advanced robots and computers to perform programmable functions on behalf of humans (although Leonardo arguably first visualized an ancient version of a robot, with his renaissance blueprints of a "robotic knight").

So, what do airplanes, robots, remote-controlled toys, and computers all have in common? With the right design, all their best elements can function together in one machine. Drones manage to put all of this technology together into one unmanned aircraft.

DRONES ON THE HOME FRONT

The word "drone" comes from *drohne*, an old German word meaning "male honeybee." In the bee kingdom, female bees make the honey and males do not. The word carries with it the connotation of idleness, laziness, and emptiness. It is not a drastic leap to see why modern scientists applied this term to pilotless aircraft: a modern drone is empty, literally.

Drones have a tremendous role to play in our present and future lives, including your education. With an estimated 100,000 drone-related jobs arising in the US economy by the year 2025 (according to the *Huffington Post*), many educational institutions are working to incorporate drones into the classrooms, into curriculum, and in other ways.

Consider all of the academic disciplines used in creating drones, and others that are enriched by their use. Engineering and mechanical know-how is required to design and build them; computer science contributes to their hardware and software; and physics and mathematics determine a drone's

THE MILITARY ORIGINS OF DRONES

Drones, as we currently understand them, have their roots in warfare. During the Vietnam War, the United States deployed drones to gather intelligence and engage in surveillance and reconnaissance. Thousands of missions were flown. These were not the hovering and maneuverable drones of today. Rather, they were more like remote-control airplanes that flew along predetermined paths.

Later, the Israeli Defense Forces (IDF) made more sophisticated drones. Many of its drones performed surveillance, but others acted as decoys in warzones. The IDF were the first to use drones to attack actual targets, including assassinations of military foes. The United States purchased Israeli drones, all the while developing their own, the first of which were only widely used during the first war between the United States and its allies and Iraq, the Gulf War in 1990.

Increasingly mobile and sophisticated drones were rolled out and used heavily after the September 11, 2001, terrorist attacks, in the subsequent war on terror and in wars waged by the United States and its allies in Afghanistan and Iraq. The military and intelligence services have used drones to perform video surveillance and reconnaissance and to target and eliminate terrorist suspects overseas, plus members and leaders of insurgent groups. These actions have inspired considerable backlash and condemnation from many of the nations where drones are used and among human rights and antiwar activists. Yet, drones remain a widely used military technology. In fact, use of drones ramped up during the antiterrorism efforts of the Barack Obama administration, despite the continued controversy.

THIS US AIR FORCE MQ-9 REAPER IS ONE OF MANY MODELS OF DRONE EMPLOYED BY THE UNITED STATES IN CONFLICT ZONES WORLDWIDE.

speed and power. A sense of invention and entrepreneurship helps other users dream up new uses for drones.

It took a great amount of research and dedication by well-trained, educated scientists and technicians to develop drones in the first place. As they become more widespread and common, educators will find more ways to use drones to help students learn. In turn, students will use their education and training to make advancements in drone technology.

A TEENAGER FLIES A QUADCOPTER. DRONE HOBBYISTS WHO LEARN ABOUT DRONES EARLY MAY GET A LEG UP ON THE REST OF THEIR PEERS, SINCE THE USE OF DRONES IN AND OUT OF CLASSROOM WILL SURELY INCREASE.

According to the Association for Unmanned Vehicles and Systems International (AUVSI), by the year 2020 there will be over 30,000 active drones in the world. The primary civilian use for them will be as farm equipment. But drones will prove useful in nearly every imaginable sphere. Teachers and students alike can use drones to advance many kinds of learning and for a myriad of academic lessons. They may become especially vital to education in science, technology, engineering and math, now commonly referred to as STEM.

DRONES FOR SCHOOLS

In 2013, the University of Illinois was awarded a K–12 STEM grant to fund the use of drones in teaching, which led to the first Drones for Schools program. Founded by mechanical engineer and journalist Matthew Schoyer, the Drones for Schools program originally sought to have students design, build, and fly drones. As a former journalist, Schoyer researched aerial robots used to cover news stories on disasters. He began building a rudimentary drone in his basement, but soon realized that teachers working for the grant were doing the same thing.

Because the grant's focus was to promote the new STEM-focused Next Generation Science Standards, Schoyer realized the students themselves should be the ones building the drones. He argued that doing so would teach students multidisciplinary lessons in an array of technical fields, including STEM subjects. Schoyer assembled a team of STEM educators and the Drones for Schools program was soon up and running.

Students applied all kinds of STEM lessons in the construction and operation of drones. They used physics and mathematics concepts to determine the drone's ideal stall speed. This is how slow certain drones can hover before they begin to freefall. Stall speed also determines the optimal power source needs. To decide on this power source, they used their instruction in physics and chemistry to choose between electrical or battery-operated motors.

They wrote code to program and create the systems that would allow them to maneuver the drone. Mathematical operations, variables, and functions all informed their hardware and software decisions. Other non-STEM subjects also guided their drone construction, like communications to market and create manuals and instructions for their drones; art and architecture to create aesthetically pleasing drone designs; and even music to manipulate the tones the drone made in flight.

Today, hundreds of schools across the country have created their own drone programs to teach any subject one can imagine: science, agriculture, technology, engineering, mathematics, art, music, journalism, photography, sports, health, law, safety, community service, and more.

DRONES ON THE COLLEGE CAMPUS

With their potential applications for many career tracks, jobs, academics, and extracurricular and leisure activities, it is no surprise that drones are also increasingly common in American higher education. In 2012, there were only 23 schools

THESE STUDENTS FROM THE UNIVERSITY OF MISSOURI ARE LEARNING HOW TO OPERATE THIS QUADCOPTER, ALONG WITH GAINING CLASSROOM INSTRUCTION IN DRONE REGULATIONS AND TECHNOLOGY.

certified to fly drones. This rose to 95 by 2016, according to the Federal Aviation Administration (FAA), and is expected to grow exponentially over the coming decade.

THE SKY'S THE LIMIT

Drone manufacturers are producing ever more advanced, fast, lightweight, and eye-pleasing models. They are being used for everything from putting on light shows, to security, to filmmaking.

With the great variety of drones that will roll out in the coming decades, there will be an equally impressive list of uses for these drones. Now is the time to become acclimated to this new technological landscape. Educators and students both can do their part to incorporate drones into learning and the school environment. Let us take a look at the present and future of drones in the classroom.

CHAPTER 2

SCIENCE, TECHNOLOGY, MATH, AND ENGINEERING (STEM)

Having a drone in the classroom is a jumping-off point for many technical subject areas. This becomes apparent as students study, design, build, test, and use drones.

GATHERING DATA

Science is grounded in observation and gathering information and data. Hypotheses that lead to theories come from (more or less) objective data. A drone's unique ability to fly over areas that are hard to access and capture accurate data make them ideal for studying science.

Imagine, for example, being assigned a project in environmental studies class to examine how manmade structures in your town co-exist alongside parts of the wild or natural world. Or you may be assigned to film examples of biodiversity. Drones can be used to map the natural terrain and features of parks, swamps, beaches, or forests. They can help students observe wildlife without disturbing it as they might do while on foot, crashing through the trees and bushes.

Such a drone-based study can serve as an amateur introduction to what professional scientists do out in the field daily. Biologists have used drones to track endangered species. Many drones have GPS built into them, which facilitates scientists' ability to track species.

ONE THING DRONES CAN DO WELL IS GATHER DATA. HERE, A DRONE IS PREPARED FOR FLIGHT OVER LIMA, PERU, TO HELP THOSE CONDUCTING RESEARCH IN AGRICULTURE AND ARCHAEOLOGY.

DRONES FOR STEM

Some drones on the retail market can be as cheap as $30 while others are $500 or higher. Generally speaking, you get what you pay for. That is, the cheaper the drone, the smaller it will tend to be, with less functionality.

The Nebraska-based organization Educational Service Unit #3 brought its Parrot Spider Mini Drone model into several schools statewide. It has spoked wheels that function as bumpers, weighs just two ounces, and costs $75. In the school gym, students programmed the drones using tablets and then sent them through obstacle courses. Using a manufactured drone allowed them to make accurate calculations that resulted in precise movements of these tiny drones through some fast-paced maneuvers, speeding through hoops, flying in and out of the gym rafters, and then halting to a stop in a box.

MAKING CALCULATIONS

When a drone is reversing, rotating, turning, or hovering, a variety of mathematical calculations and physics concepts are at play, which teachers can highlight for their students. For example, out on the same Nebraskan school's sports fields, students who had built air rockets used the same drones to capture aerial images of where the rockets landed. This data was used to calculate and compare the rockets' trajectories, a core physics concept focused on calculating the curved path of a flying object.

A PARROT MINIDRONE—THIS ONE KNOWN AS THE "ROLLING SPIDER" — FLIES DURING A DEMONSTRATION IN NEW YORK. THIS SMALL DRONE CAN FLY LIKE A HELICOPTER AND IS CONTROLLED BY A SMARTPHONE.

Other ideas for experiments might include using different-size drones to perform similar tasks in different environments and analyzing the resulting differences in their performance, including their trajectory and effectiveness.

Having a drone in the STEM classroom creates many avenues for bringing traditional science and math lessons to life. Drones can assist in tasks such as measuring temperatures, detecting materials in the air, and monitoring environmental and agricultural conditions. Some elementary school teachers have found ways to bring decimals and the x/y axis to life through the use of drones in the classroom. Students fly the drone for a specific time such as 4.2 seconds and program them to move up the y axis and along the x axis for this amount of time.

LEARNING BY DOING: MAKING YOUR OWN DRONE

If your school does not have the budget for manufactured drones, or if you (or your teacher) are more interested in figuring out things from the ground up, making a drone as a class project can teach a whole range of cross-curricular STEM concepts.

Drones are especially popular among young people because they are new and innovative. While students do learn many crucial aspects of technology from textbooks and memorization, the opportunity to design, build, program, and operate drones is an exciting one for young learners because it is almost entirely a hands-on process. It also demonstrates quite visibly to students how theoretical ideas and plans can be translated into something actual and concrete—that can then do some very cool tricks, too!

Building drones from component parts, or even devising simple parts from scratch, can be the basis of a course of study many that schools tossed aside in recent decades, but which may be making a comeback: shop class. Drone design and assembly may serve as a jumping-off point for basic robotics, engineering, industrial design, and other technical

TWO STUDENTS BUILD A DRONE TOGETHER IN AN AFTER-SCHOOL ENGINEERING CLUB. DRONE ASSEMBLY MAY SERVE AS A JUMPING-OFF POINT FOR STUDENTS TO ENTER VARIOUS TECHNICAL FIELDS.

pursuits. In addition, students who have expressed an interest in learning a trade (such as future electricians) may particularly benefit from drone-building classes.

IN BUILDING AND ENGINEERING

Other innovative applications of drones have been tried out in the realm of architecture and building. For example, in 2013, a team of architects and roboticists working together at the Swiss Federal Institute of Technology in Zurich, Switzerland, programed drones to spool cable behind them as they flew to create structures high up in the air, far above the heads of people or traditional building equipment. Project leader Federico Augugliaro told *New Scientist*, "Flying machines have an unlimited workspace—they can go anywhere . . . They can move parts to any location and fly in and around existing structures."

These kinds of drones can provide exciting tools for younger students to learn the basics of building structures, including simple buildings, and bridges. Students can command drones to fly simultaneously to create knots and other combinations that make their constructions strong and stable.

A DIY MOVEMENT

Do-it-yourself (DIY) drone construction has a niche place in the current maker movement popular among teens and adults. This movement encourages participants to embrace their inner inventor, eschewing purchased gadgets in favor of things they have made themselves, including drones. The maker movement nurtures qualities that students and professionals in STEM need: inventiveness, risk-taking, proactivity, and good old-fashioned curiosity, the mother of all invention.

DRONES FOR TECH JOBS

Educators hope that drone-based lessons will promote future high-tech jobs. For example, a special education class in a California school is geared toward training students for the

DRONES 101: GETTING HANDS-ON

In 2015, eleven schools in Florida received grants from Embry Riddle Aeronautics University and Florida Farm Bureau via the Future Farmers of America to teach students agricultural operations using unmanned aircraft systems, according to the *Sun-Sentinel*. In addition to instructing students in the physics and chemistry concepts involved in operating the drones, students get lessons in agriculture by learning how to snap aerial photos of crops in order to identify and diagnose issues.

One school, South Plantation High in Plantation, Florida, launched one of the first drone-centered classes in the state with money from this venture. Students and teachers have been extremely enthusiastic about it. "If you've ever flown a drone, it's the most exciting thing ever," teacher Gustavo Junco told the *Sun-Sentinel*. "We're teaching the kids how to fly drones safely and how to build them and how to computer program them as well."

The school's collection of drones now ranges from simple, small ones with a retail price tag of less than $100, to a $5,000 model known as the Inspire, by DJI, a Chinese manufacturer that is arguably the biggest producer of drones. Students not only handle the drones, but also learn about their history and become familiar with the regulatory and legal landscape surrounding drones, including the rules restricting their use. These include the ever-changing but still restrictive rules from the FAA, such as drones being required to stay below 400 feet (122 m), and at least 5 miles (8 km) from an airport or airfield. At the end of their course, the students have to study and pass a written exam that lasts an hour and a half. This gives them industry certification in flying drones safely.

In Annapolis, Maryland, school administrators have also come to consider courses in drone technology as one future path for traditional shop and information technology (IT) education. They teach students to submit business plans for their drones' use, how to operate 3D printing technology to adapt their drones, and how to pilot them. In Mount Olive, New Jersey, a high school media class has purchased several drone models for use in its student-produced TV show. Everywhere, classes focused on drones are taking off.

technology jobs of the future. One part of the curriculum is learning basic code that controls the movement of a robot. Students then learn how to apply this basic knowledge to the more complex mechanics of drones. Despite the challenges of navigating the world with special needs, this group of students has embraced STEM lessons centered around drones.

SCIENCE FAIRS AND COMPETITIONS

Drones have become popular at science fairs. With his entry to the Google Science Fair, held online, one student from Pittsburgh, Mihir Garimella, won top honors in the category for 13–14 year olds with a drone-centered project. Garimella was interested in programing a drone to evade obstacles, both moving and nonmoving. He was inspired to tackle this project when he saw fruit flies circling a fruit bowl on a counter in his kitchen and saw how easily they evaded being swatted. He then researched the fruit fly's biology—particularly its simple form of vision—and used that information to mimic its movements, creating an algorithm to replicate these. His drone was able to dodge first horizontally, then vertically, in the process of avoiding threats.

From Dubai to Silicon Valley, drone competitions are becoming a popular pasttime and learning experience. The 2015 California State Fair hosted the first national drone

High school instructors are finding creative ways to incorporate drones into their classes. Shop teachers, media instructors, and teachers in the agricultural sciences can teach lessons using drones.

racing competition and the top prize went to an Australian contestant. A teenager from the United Kingdom took the top prize at the March 2016 World Drone Prix in Dubai.

Students around the country are enjoying their own school-sponsored races in gyms and football fields. Participating in drone-based STEM competitions, as well as finding ways to build or use drones in STEM classes now, will give students a competitive advantage as they enter the college and career years.

MONEY FOR GRANTS

Every year, the AUVSI offers middle and high school students hands-on robotics activities and competitions that promote STEM fields. More than $1.4 million has been given away since the competitions began in 1991. From Virginia to China, the foundation hosts up to eight competitions each year. In the foundation-sponsored National SeaPerch Challenge, student teams demonstrate underwater UAV ability in underwater obstacle courses. Its annual Student Unmanned Aerial Systems Competition (SUAS) requires students to create, implement, record, and report on a drone that is capable of autonomous flight and navigation.

CHAPTER 3

DRONES IN MEDIA AND THE HUMANITIES

T he ability of drones to go nearly anywhere makes them invaluable. Their unique capability to access those hard-to-reach places, climb to great heights and hover, swoop over landscapes, and film or photograph everything below, makes them ideal as teaching aids in multimedia and journalism, as well as many liberal arts subjects.

Some institutions of higher education with drone-related instruction offer courses that focus mostly on how to properly engage in aerial photography and use drones to capture video footage. From the images of the destruction left behind by a 2014 tornado in Arkansas to aerial footage of the Apple Campus under construction, modern media outlets depend on the high-quality images of current events that drones can capture from heretofore unattainable vantage points.

Obtaining these images poses little risk to the humans operating the drones safely from the ground, a major reason for their increasing popularity for school use. Versatile drone technology can help humanities students produce quality, eye-catching content; help in newsgathering for student journalists; assist with digital yearbooks; and provide a host of other new and exciting possibilities for students in many different subject areas.

A DRONE OPERATOR PREPARES TO LAUNCH HIS DEVICE IN THE CALIFORNIA DESERT. HANDS-ON, OUTDOOR INSTRUCTION IN DRONE USE CAN TAKE STUDENTS OUT OF THE CLASSROOM AND INTO THE EXCITING OUTDOORS.

FILM AND MULTIMEDIA PRODUCTION

A revolution has been slowly occurring since the 1990s, when digital cameras allowed for cheaper and high-quality images for cinema and television. By the 2000s, even smartphones had reached a level of recording quality that rivaled that of professional equipment.

The newest revolution in film incorporates the mobility and flexibility of the drone. High school students, often the most savvy early adopters of such technologies, stand to

THIS QUADCOPTER IS EQUIPPED WITH A GOPRO CAMERA, ONE OF MANY PHOTOGRAPHIC TOOLS NOW DESIGNED TO CAPTURE IMAGES AND FOOTAGE WHILE MOVING, WHICH MAKE THEM IDEAL FOR USE WITH DRONES.

embrace and leverage the power of drones to create works of art and media never seen before.

In recent years, student-filmed projects ranging from video reenactments of famous local historical events to video blogs (vlogs) of field trips have found their way onto YouTube, Vimeo, Facebook, Twitter, Vine, and other online video sharing platforms.

IN ART

Drones have a versatile quality that lends itself to artistic expression. Because you can attach paint brushes, cables, and other tools and multimedia materials to drones, many art teachers recognize this versatility and have introduced drones into the curriculum to produce works of art. Because they can move independently, drones may also be used in creative works in new and innovative ways.

If they lay a large sheet of paper outside on the grass and attach paintbrushes to drones, students can lower them into paint buckets and then randomly splash and drop paint onto the canvas. This method can teach abstract art techniques. Or, if the students apply paint more systematically and methodically, then the lesson can cover more specific art techniques such as shading and patterning. Once individual students get the hang of these techniques, they can collaborate to produce large murals on walls, pavement, and other large school surfaces using coordinated drone movements.

THIS AERIAL VIEW OF THE ROCK FORMATIONS AT KALFASTROND IN LAKE MYVATN, ICELAND, WAS SHOT USING A DRONE. JOURNALISTS REGULARLY RELY ON DRONES TO CAPTURE UNIQUE AND NEWSWORTHY IMAGERY.

DRONE JOURNALISM

The Professional Society of Drone Journalists (PSDJ) declares its mission to foster and develop ways to use UAVs for the purpose of gathering newsworthy stories. PSDJ maintains that the public's access to information is limited when journalists who use drones are banned from areas where there are breaking stories. At the same time, PSDJ recognizes that there is a "hierarchy of ethics" when it comes to reporting on news with a drone's help. The top two considerations in this hierarchy are newsworthiness and safety, followed by national drone laws, privacy, and traditional journalistic ethics.

As aerial platforms for gathering data such as counting attendance at sports events or documenting violent uprisings in Egypt and Afghanistan, drones have enabled independent journalists to safely participate in breaking news stories in ways that were impossible to do previously without putting themselves directly in harm's way.

Drones will surely become ever more popular among budding journalists who are interested in gathering news but may be too inexperienced (or simply too young) to cover certain events safely (or legally) up close. They can thus provide an entry point for those just learning the ropes.

Teenage journalists and commentators, empowered by the reach, ease of use, and more or less free usage of social media platforms like Tumblr, as well as video-sharing platforms and blogs, will no longer need an institution to report on news in their communities. School journalism and media teachers can help them adhere to standard newsgathering ethics when reporting on local news—emergencies, protests, civic matters—while also giving them pointers on how to utilize drones to gather footage. They can do this while making sure they do not violate local ordinances, interfere with the work of law enforcement or first responders, or prevent paid journalism professionals from doing their jobs.

There is little substitute for being on the scene in the heat of the action when you are an adult professional in the news business. But young people can add drones to the list of ways they can ease into this dynamic career path.

SHOPPING FOR DRONES

In October 2015, an online post from the New York Film Academy (NYFA) reviewed several of the best drones available for purchase for student cinematographers, filmmaking teachers, and even hobbyists and amateur aficionados. These included:

- The DJI Inspire I: Weighing in at 6.4 pounds (2.9 kg), and costing about $2,800, NYFA's reviewer declared this drone "the go-to, professional drone for 4K aerial photography." The term 4K refers to 4,000 pixels of resolution displayed in finished footage. It can fly for a maximum of 18 minutes and achieve a speed of 48 mph (77 kph), with a maximum altitude of 14,763 feet (4,500 m). One benefit to the DJI Inspire that partly makes up for its price tag is its flexibility. It can be modified and upgraded easily, eliminating the need to buy other drones for a long time.
- The DJI Phantom 3 Advanced: This drone costs $999 and weighs 2.8 pounds (1.28 kg). It can fly for 23 minutes at a speed of 35 mph (56 kph), and to the height of 19,685 feet (6,000 m). Its camera makes images at 2.7K pixels
- The Parrot Bebop: At $500, this .92-pound (420 g) drone can fly for 22 minutes at about 29 mph (47 kph), at up to 200 meters (656 feet), and with 1080 pixel recording. NYFA said it was a "a smart choice for those who want HD stabilized video without having to spend a king's ransom."

Even cheaper drones are available for schools and students on a budget, including: the Sky Viper ($99 with a 720-pixel camera); the UDI RC 818A Quadcopter for $85, which is considered great for children and beginners; the super-cheap $40 Hubsan X4 H107C; and many others.

HISTORY AND SOCIAL STUDIES

Two more subject areas in which students can use drones to enhance their homework and projects are social studies and history. Local history can be brought to life with video essays that tour notable landmarks and historical sites, including ones that are common destinations for teachers and students.

For example, a student living in or visiting Philadelphia, Pennsylvania—perhaps even during a school trip—can illustrate the process of the Thirteen Colonies becoming a united, independent nation with drone-enabled imagery of famous historical sites from the colonial and Revolutionary War eras, such as Independence Hall, the Liberty Bell, and Carpenters' Hall.

Students of urban planning might guide a drone through a city center into first-ring suburbs, then distant suburbs, and eventually the countryside to record the changing buildings and landscape. Another idea is to map the same area at different times, especially as development occurs, to show how the built landscape transforms over time.

Yet another fascinating project idea is to stage a large reenactment of a famous event. You can recruit fellow students to set up and film a portrayal of notable historical milestones, such as famous battles and speeches. Another option is to visit historical sites where professional re-enactors are staging large events with many participants. This is common among Civil War history buffs, who dress up in 19th-century military gear and

STUDENTS USE DRONES TO FILM HISTORIC SITES. HOWEVER, THEY SHOULD RESEARCH LOCAL REGULATIONS. FOR EXAMPLE, THERE IS A BAN ON FLYING NEAR THE EIFFEL TOWER IN PARIS, FRANCE, AND MANY OTHER MONUMENTS.

enact the Battle of Gettysburg and other crucial events. The possibilities for documenting one's immediate region are endless. This includes researching nearby state or national parks, monuments, or attractions.

Students can even get involved in local development and civic issues via drone recordings of their neighborhood, town, city, county, or region. These recordings can then be used to create presentations that advocate for necessary improvements to their communities. Students concerned about food deserts—the absence of good stores where residents can buy produce and healthful foods—might film their neighborhood to highlight this lack of resources, and present the information in edited form to a town or city council.

Other students might engage with and try to influence their local government on other matters that concern them, including unfair allocations of parkland, medical facilities, and law enforcement resources. Teachers and administrators can help with such projects and point student leaders in the right direction to connect with those who have influence over such matters.

Naturally, any student-organized or initiated projects involving drones should be supervised by adults, including parents, teachers, and other authority figures. It is up to those who are the legal age (in most states, 18 years of age) to have responsible adults sign any relevant paperwork or permissions. They should not rely only on adults, however, to research these rules and regulations, but reach out to relevant authorities and parties themselves. This will give them a lesson on how to engage with government and bureaucracies while figuring out the ways they can use and learn with drones safely and legally.

CHAPTER 4

OUTSIDE OF THE CLASSROOM

Drones are not only becoming part of many classrooms and core curricula but also may soon be used for school tasks. Football, track, and PE coaches can rely on them for accurate footage of practices. School administrators, staff, teachers, and students may all use drones to record various school events for archival or promotional purposes. Their role in school security is in its infancy, as school boards, principals, and politicians everywhere consider their efficacy in helping keep students and staff safe.

SCHOOL SPORTS

One of the most dynamic uses for drones in recent years is their incorporation into school sports. In football practice, coaches can use drones to analyze plays, test formations, learn from breakdowns in communication, and even program drones to perform some electronic referee functions. Since drones are allowed up to 400 feet (123 meters) in the air, their birds-eye-view can be ideal for field-based sports like football, lacrosse, and soccer. Under some circumstances, they may even be employed within gymnasiums, though many institutions may not allow drones indoors due to the danger of malfunction or operator error that could result in injuries, and even death.

THIS FOOTBALL FIELD IN ANDOVER, MASSACHUSETTS, WAS PHOTOGRAPHED BY A DRONE. THE BIRD'S EYE VIEW PROVIDED BY DRONES IS IDEAL FOR COVERAGE OF FIELD-BASED SPORTS.

ON THE FIELD, ON THE ROAD

In a single view, coaches can track all the moves that team members make, and how their actions help or hinder a team's overall performance. Cameras rigged to cables, end zones, or camera towers provide much of this field perspective already. However, only a drone can hover 15 feet (5 m) above a player's head and give precise detail on foot and hand placement, and then immediately follow this with a quick zoom up to give data on spacing between all of the players on the field.

It is this maneuverability of drones that makes them useful for monitoring the quick and dynamic play of both team sports and other athletic disciplines. However, just as we must balance privacy and safety concerns against the use of drones in society, educators must also consider the privacy and safety of students and staff before determining the roles for drones in their schools.

For example, Cleveland.com reported in late 2015 that the Ohio High School Athletic Association (OHSAA) was trying to work out new regulations on drones being used at high school sporting events. At that time, drones were prohibited at high school tournaments for any sport, and each school was responsible for making up rules as to whether they would allow them in regular-season play. Host sites that allowed drones were responsible for assuming all legal liability arising from drone usage, and also for making sure that any local, state, or federal regulations were followed.

One issue was how referees and teams would react to drones that interfered with game play. Drones might distract

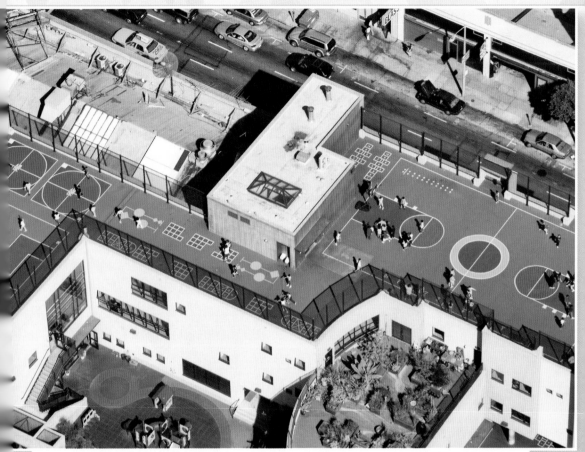

THIS AERIAL VIEW OF A SCHOOL ROOFTOP PLAYGROUND IN SAN FRANCISCO, CALIFORNIA, DEMONSTRATES THE KIND OF SURVEILLANCE DRONES CAN PROVIDE TO SECURITY STAFF AND LAW ENFORCEMENT.

tation can get in on the action by using drones to check that their child has been picked up or arrived safely. Some schools in Belgium recently experimented with allowing drones to provide surveillance during exams or as unannounced safety check-ins in the classroom.

DRONES: BEST FRIEND OR BIG BROTHER?

Drones might become an integral part of our school environments and in our society at large. However, their surveillance abilities pose serious ethical concerns. Their benefits for security and for helping law enforcement are countered by potential abuses, some of them quite harrowing, critics warn.

Proponents point out that drones can help secure schools by alerting teachers and administrators to fights, bullying, vandalism, and general delinquency. Their potential in helping to discover quickly, assess, and defuse even more dangerous situations—fires and other accidental perils, as well mass shootings and hostage situations—is evident. Drones can get onto a school campus that is on lockdown with far greater ease and more safely than first responders. According to *Campus Safety Magazine*, "Drones can easily monitor wide swaths of hard-to-reach and high-risk locations, such as trails and parking lots, while also providing all first responders with real-time situational awareness during campus emergencies."

Critics of drone use at school counter that constant surveillance can easily cross the line, and end up treating students as little better than institutional prisoners. Students' exposure to constant monitoring is normalized over time, contributing to a future society that is over-policed, punitive, and fear-oriented. The ability of next-generation drones to peek into private areas like locker rooms and showers also troubles many critics.

The American Civil Liberties Union (ACLU), an influential legal advocacy group, recognizes the benefits of drones, but maintains that if they are "deployed without proper regulation, drones equipped with facial recognition software, infrared technology, and speakers capable of monitoring personal conversations would cause unprecedented invasions of our privacy rights." As they have proliferated in American life, many critics fear drones' presence has become intrusive and threatening.

OUTDOORS AT SCHOOL

The aerial footage that drones supply to the school sports teams can also support other large-scale outdoor school events. For example, school marching bands rely on precise formations of their band members to create images such as the school's initials or superhero logos. Drone footage of their attempts at these shapes can help band directors fine-tune the performance. Watching from the bleachers can provide limited aerial views but the options are limitless for a drone that can zoom in and dart out above the band members' heads. The same is true for dance teams, flag corps, cheerleaders, and other groups that integrate formations into their performances.

High schools that wish to promote their sports teams, school campus, or student programs might use a drone to

DRONES CAN CAPTURE SCHOOL EVENTS AND SCENES, SUCH AS GRADUATION DAY OR SCHOOL LANDMARKS, TO CREATE PROMOTIONAL OR ARCHIVAL VIDEO.

capture promotional video. This is becoming more prevalent as a marketing tool for private schools, universities recruiting new students, and other institutions. They can use drones to showcase campus buildings, dormitories, or attractive and well-manicured campus landscapes.

CHAPTER 5

THE FUTURE OF DRONES IN EDUCATION

Drones have tremendous potential for modern education and in many future career tracks. Future college students, technologists, media specialists, filmmakers, and military servicemen and women all stand to benefit from getting in on the ground floor of drone technology and use.

CURRENT AND FUTURE TECHNOLOGY

Cutting-edge drone manufacturers are bringing ever-diverse models, offering more utility as educational tools. German-based drone research firm Drone Industry

Insights, recently compiled data on the top 20 registered drone types in the United States in 2015 and reports that the lightweight, camera-wielding DJI Phantom (about 2.8 pounds and $2500) is the number one drone.

In contrast, the twentieth spot was taken by one of the heaviest and most expensive quadcopter models available: Lockheed Martin's Indago weighing in at nearly 5 pounds and costing $25,000. The Phantom is geared toward new drone users and hobbyists while the Indago caters to multiple sectors: civilian, commercial, and military. Because innovation in the drone market includes both hobbyists and drones for professional applications,

A DRONE IS FLOWN FOR RECREATIONAL PURPOSES AS AN AIRPLANE PASSES OVERHEAD IN THE SKY ABOVE OLD BETHPAGE, NEW YORK.

manufacturers are innovating their original models in both spheres.

Drone cameras are becoming more powerful, their controls more precise, and software applications more versatile and sophisticated. Drones will also be developed with incredible sensitivity to the orders issued from their operators.

COLLEGE AND CAREER TRAINING WITH DRONES

Countless pilot training schools are integrating drones into the curriculum. From well-known technical institutions such as Embry Riddle Aeronautics University to liberal arts schools like the Christian Liberty University—which recently added an Unmanned Aircraft Systems (UAS) program—many colleges, universities, and technical schools offer UAV certification as part of aeronautics degrees and other majors. These schools prepare students for careers piloting a drone, becoming an aerial drone photographer, or working as a UAV systems engineer, among other career tracks. In addition to aeronautics and the military programs, innovative programs in industries such as journalism and agriculture are integrating drones into their student training.

As such programs become more ubiquitous and popular, it is likely that high school preparatory courses and instruction that familiarize students with drones will also become commonplace. Drone-building seminars, clubs, and drone-oriented shop-type classes will teach students the basics of drone design, construction, programming, and flight.

Drones of the future that get larger may be used to deliver packages and other payloads. Smaller drones will be created for ever more discrete surveillance, as well as many helpful and useful applications that we have yet to see fully exploited.

MAKING CONNECTIONS AND GETTING ORGANIZED

Professionals who use drones in their industries today are getting organized. The Association for Unmanned Vehicles and Systems International is working to advance employ-

COLLEGE STUDENTS WORK ON MECHANICAL DRONES FOR AN ENGINEERING PROJECT. THERE ARE MANY PROFESSIONAL ORGANIZATIONS AND AMATEUR CLUBS DEDICATED TO DRONES.

ment opportunities and training for the UAV community, and to help change the legal and regulatory landscape to favor drone use and proliferation.

InterDrone, the international drone conference and exposition, is now a major annual conference that supports three sectors: drone entrepreneurs and developers (Drone-Tech Con); business, sales, and commercial enterprises (Drone Enterprise); and film professionals (Drone Cinema). In 2015, InterDrone convened 2,800 drone builders, flyers, and buyers from 48 countries and all US states for a conference. Another important drone meet-up is the Drone World Expo, which concentrates on the commercial applications of drone technology.

DRONES AND ECONOMIC GROWTH

There are many job sectors and industries that are working to incorporate drones soon or in the more distant future. Students who study up on the variety of uses for drones in various industries, both private and public (government), will be better equipped to thrive in drone-related fields

AGRICULTURE

In many areas of the United States where agriculture is still a major livelihood, local high schools often offer courses that will prepare graduates for farm work or for college and trade-school coursework in the agricultural sciences. Drones use remote sensors to pinpoint health problems and disease outbreaks in crops, assess proper hydration for crops, and analyze soil quality, pests, and other factors.

Drones are also being adapted to distribute nutrients, pesticides, and to perform other agricultural tasks. Modern students of agriculture will be as likely to have to learn drone programming and maintenance as to learn to properly sow fields. Unmanned aerial vehicles will help manage livestock herds, assessing necessary food and water distribution.

CONSTRUCTION, BUILDING, AND OTHER TRADES

Young people interested in the building and construction trades, which will utilize drones in many capacities, should also get a leg up on drone technology. Drones will be used extensively to inspect buildings for safety and structural integrity, check on supplies and construction progress, survey landscapes and potential sites, and in many other ways.

Many school districts are resurrecting shop classes and vocational-technical education. Students who have the ear of their teachers, guidance counselors, and parents (who can advocate on their behalf), should encourage their schools to begin or strengthen a shop class curriculum with drones. Metal shop instructors can easily incorporate drone building into their lesson planning. The Maker Movement has influenced many designers of school curricula to incorporate Maker-related coursework, and drones fit well with that innovative trend.

AERIAL INTERNET

This industry is still its infancy—it actually does not exist yet. One of its original proponents is Facebook CEO Mark Zuckerberg. Zuckerberg proposed a plan to use solar-powered drones to provide high-speed Internet access to everyone on the planet. These would act as mini-satellites and servers that could provide Internet connections to underserved, distant, or rural areas from high elevations. Students can implement a small-scale version of this idea by networking a few small, cheap, and Bluetooth-capable drones together to created a movable and wireless network.

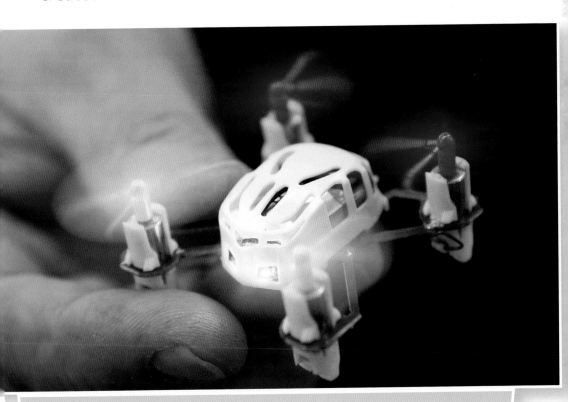

A REPRESENTATIVE OF A CHINESE UAV MANUFACTURER SHOWCASES A MICRODRONE AT A TECHNOLOGY FAIR IN HANOVER, GERMANY.

DRONES: TAKING OFF

Stemfinity.com reports over 1,000 STEM grants for schools available in all 50 states, many of which are dedicated to promoting drone use and technology. AUSVI's 2013 economic report predicts that the integration of drones into the stock market will reach $13.6 billion by 2018 and will hit the $82.1 billion mark between 2018 and 2025. By 2025, there will be approximately 103,776 new drone jobs created.

Projections for new drones, especially in educational contexts, continue to favor faster, lighter, multi-functional models. These have the most diverse uses across sectors, including education, as they can easily bounce between extreme heights and extreme close-ups to provide the accurate data that is conducive to good research. Whether you are interested in STEM classes, liberal arts, sports, or are still discovering your interests, drones will likely play a role in your education.

By the time you have finished school, a thriving market for drone uses and technology will exist that promises unlimited opportunities for your future. Studying drones now will make your school years more exciting, and your future prospects more alluring. Your future is looking up and it is abuzz with drones.

GLOSSARY

AERONAUTICS The science dealing with the operation of aircraft.

CINEMATOGRAPHY The artform of motion picture photography.

CONDUCIVE Tending to promote or assist something.

DIY Stands for "do-it-yourself," a creative philosophy in which practitioners make things without professional assistance.

ENTREPRENEUR A person who starts a business or other profit-making enterprise.

HARROWING Extremely disturbing or distressing; grievous and destructive.

INTRUSIVE Describes something that is unwanted or unwelcome, especially when it come to one's personal space or privacy.

MANEUVERABILITY The ability to easily make a series of changes in direction and position.

MULTIMEDIA Using more than one medium of expression or communication such as combining sound, video, and text to express ideas.

PROPONENT One who argues in favor of something.

QUADCOPTER A multi-rotor helicopter or drone that typically uses two clockwise and two counterclockwise fixed propellers.

ROBOT A machine that performs human-like actions or tasks.

RUDIMENTARY Describing something of basic, primitive, or imperfect design.

SECTOR A sociological, economic, or political subdivision of society.

STEM Acronym standing for science, technology, engineering, and mathematics, grouped in contrast to the study of the humanities.

TRAJECTORY A physics term used for the path of something moving, incuding a flying object.

TRUANT Someone who is absent from school without permission.

UAV Acronym that stands for unmanned aerial vehicle. UAVs can be remote-controlled or fly autonomously via pre-programmed flight plans; synonym for drone.

FOR MORE INFORMATION

Academy of Model Aeronautics (AMA)
5161 E. Memorial Dr.
Muncie, IN 47302
(800) 435-9262
Website: http://www.modelaircraft.org
Established in 1936, the AMA is the world's largest model aviation association whose mission is to promote the development of model aviation as a recognized sport and recreation activity.

Association for Unmanned Vehicles and Systems International (AUVSI)
2700 S. Quincy Street, Suite 400
Arlington, VA 22206
United States
(703) 845-9671
Website: http://www.auvsi.org/home
The Association for Unmanned Vehicles and Systems International is the world's largest nonprofit organization devoted to advancing unmanned systems and robotics.

Canadian Centre for Unmanned Vehicle Systems
#4, 49 Viscount Avenue SW
Medicine Hat, Alberta, Canada T1A5G4
(403) 488-7208
Website: http://www.ccuvs.com
CCUVS is a federally registered nonprofit whose purpose is to facilitate sustained growth in the Canadian civil and commercial unmanned systems sector.

WEBSITES

Because of the changing nature of internet links, Rosen Publishing has developed an online list of websites related to the subject of this book. This site is updated regularly. Please use this link to access this list:

http://www.rosenlinks.com/IWD/class

Levy, Leah. "What Drone Technology Can Teach Students." Edudemic. October 27, 2015. http://www.edudemic.com/drones-classroom-can-happen.

Menard, Drew. "Navigating The Future of Drone Training." *Liberty Journal*, February 17, 2016. https://www.liberty.edu/journal/article/navigating-the-future-of -drone-training.

Minor, John. "Advances in Drone Technology Will Revolutionize Campus Security." *Campus Safety*, February 2, 2016. http://www.campussafetymagazine.com/ article/advances_in_drone_technology_will_revolutionize_campus_security/ Drone.

Oneal, David. "NJ High School Uses Drones in Classroom." *That Drone Show*, November 25, 2014. http://www.thatdroneshow.com/nj-high-school-uses- drones-classroom.

Osborne, Charlie. "Drones 101 Takes to US Classrooms." ZDnet.com, December 11, 2013. http://www.zdnet.com/article/drones-101-takes-to-us-classrooms.

RC Flight Line.com. "History of Radio Control." Retrieved March 15, 2016. https:// rcflightline.com/rc-history.

Robohub.org. "Drones for Schools Program." Retrieved March 16, 2016. http:// robohub.org/drones-for-schools.

Sanctis, Matt. "Students Using Drones to Learn High-tech Jobs Dayton Daily News." *Dayton Daily News*, March 13, 2014. http://www.daytondailynews.com/ news/news/local-education/students-using-drones-to-learn-high-tech-jobs/ nfCRs.

Science Kids.co.nz. "History of Robotics." Retrieved March 7, 2016. http://www .sciencekids.co.nz/sciencefacts/technology/historyofrobotics.html.

Shammas, Brittany. "Learning Takes Flight in South Plantation High Drone Class." *Sun-Sentinel*, April 15, 2016. http://www.sun-sentinel.com/local/broward/fl -broward-drone-class-20160414-story.html.

Teamedtech.com. "Using Drones in the Classroom." Retrieved March 17, 2016. http://teamedtech.com/index.php/2015/05/25/best-drones-for-the-classroom.

Turk, John. "Taking Flight: Brandon High School Teacher Creates Drone Program to 'Put Students Ahead of the Curve.'" *The Oakland Press*, April 28, 2015. http:// www.theoaklandpress.com/article/OP/20150428/NEWS/150429406.

WCJB.com. "High School Students Learn to Fly Drones." December 10, 2015. http:// www.wcjb.com/morning-edition-local-news/2015/12/high-school-students -learn-fly-drones.

INDEX

A

aerial internet, 55
Aero Trainer, 44
agriculture, 13, 20, 53–54
art, 14, 29, 31
Augugliaro, Federico, 23

B

buildings and construction, 17, 22–25, 54–55

C

careers and employment, 9, 14, 23–25, 33, 53–55, 56
coding, 14, 25
colleges and universities, 13, 14–16, 28, 51
community events, 14, 35–37, 43
conferences, 52–53
creating drones, 21–22, 54–55

D

Da Vinci, Leonardo, 7, 9
Drone Cinema, 53
Drone Enterprise, 53
Drone Industry Insights, 50
Drone Journalists, Professional Society of (PSDJ), 32
Drones for Schools program, 13–14
Drone Tech-Con, 53
Drone World Expo, 53

E

economic impact, 9, 53–56
Educational Service Unit #3, 17

Embry Riddle Aeronautics University, 24, 51
environmental applications, 17–18, 20
ethical concerns, 10, 32–33, 46–47

F

Federal Aviation Administration, 16, 24, 43
film and photography, 14, 28–29, 30–31, 51, 53
first responders, 33, 46–47
Fitbit, 44
funding and grants, 27, 56

G

Garimella, Mihir, 26–27

H

health, 14, 43–44
high schools, 19, 24–25, 54
history and social studies, 35–37

I

Illinois, University of, 13
Indago, 50
Inspire, 26–27, 34
intelligence gathering, 10
Interdrone, 53

J

journalism, 14, 28–29, 32–33

L

law enforcement, 46–47
Liberty University, 51
Lockheed Martin, 50

M

Maker Movement, 23, 54
mapping, 16
marching bands, 47
marketing, 47–48
media, 28–29, 30–31
military technology, 8, 10
music, 14, 47

P

Parrot Bebop, 34
Parrot Spider Mini Drone, 17
Phantom drones, 34, 50
physical education, 43–44
power sources, 14, 55
prices, 19, 24, 34, 50
primary schools, 20–21

Q

quadcopters, 34, 50

R

regulation, 25, 33, 37, 40–41, 53
robots, 8–9,
rockets, 19

S

safety, 14, 33, 44–45, 46
Schoyer, Matthew, 13
science fairs, 25–27
science, technology, engineering, and
    math education (STEM), 9, 13–14,
    19–22, 23
social media, 31
Special Education, 23–25

sports, 14, 19, 33, 38–43
stall speeds, 14
surveillance, 10, 46–47
Swiss Federal Institute of Technology,
    22–23

U

Unmanned Vehicles and Systems Inter-
    national, Association for (AUVSI), 13,
    27, 51, 56
urban planning, 35–37

W

weather, 20
wildlife, 18

Y

yearbooks, 29, 42

Z

Zuckerberg, Mark, 55

ABOUT THE AUTHOR

Katherine Yaun has a Master's degree in English and teaches ESL at a university in Florida. She is also a writer and editor and has covered many topics in her career including education, literature, and travel. Katherine has worked for educational agencies and taught English internationally. She has learned about educational and technology trends in these settings, particularly when working to develop postsecondary STEM exams under a federal grant. This is her third Rosen book.

PHOTO CREDITS